The Church of Milk and Honey

A Year of Collective Wisdom
Compiled by Gwen Van Velsor

Contributing Authors

Week 1: Gwen Van Velsor

Week 2: Maria C. Goodson

Week 3: Ann Quinn

Week 4: Amy Hoogs

Week 5: Loree Edwards

Week 6: Kathleen Van Velsor

Week 7: Carol Clupny

Week 8: Patty Blank

Week 9: Maria C. Goodson

Week 10: Kara Panowitz

Week 11-16: Jannica Cuaresma Breslin

Week 17: Giuse Varni

Week 18: Kristie Graybill

Week 19: Gina Strauss

Week 20: Marylou Fusco

Week 21: Nicole Shea

Week 22: Galen Peterson

Week 23: Jannica Cuaresma Breslin

Week 24: Rosanne Shank

Week 25: Kristen Zory King

Week 26: Nancy Carver Wade

Week 27: Anonymous

Week 28: Sonia Martinez

Week 29: Joan van Velsor

Week 30: Kristen Zory King

Week 31: Emily J. Telfair Hadley

Week 32: Jan Woodcock

Week 33: Siobhan McKenna

Week 34: Jannica Cuaresma Breslin

Week 35: Rosanne Shank

Week 36: Kapua Iao

Week 37: Ava Van Velsor

Week 38: Sam Anthony

Week 39: Anna Manning-Launius

Week 40: Jan Woodcock

Week 41: Robyn Maggio

Week 42: Gwen Van Velsor

Week 43: Jannica Cuaresma Breslin

Week 44: Jessica Cho Johnston

Week 45–48: Mary Speace

Week 49: Carol Clupny

Week 50: Jannica Cuaresma Breslin

Week 51: Gwen Van Velsor

Week 52: You

To all those who have come before and all those who will come after. We hold space for you today.

To Begin With
By Gwen Van Velsor

I gaze at my snow globe life and mull over the months of the year, the hours in a day, the decades curling up at my heels. I once thought, ah I will write, I will create, and something may come of that or something may not and at least it will be a good try and at least there will be some permanent product of my existence.

And then as the pages rolled off the presses and books made their way into hands a stillness came over the head-hand-heart triangle of creation and I saw that it wasn't the words at all but the fingerprint connections between my soul and yours. Each time you walked with me and my stories we pressed our hands together to make something new. And each time we touched I learned something.

I am no more a writer than a collector. No more a collector than a seeker. No more a seeker than a dreamer. And no more a dreamer than a life of breath, of change, of stillness, of love. These words are not my words, they are our words, knitted together over a collection of experiences.

And I realize now, this is who I am, a collection of experiences with all of you. Blessed or bruised, you are the ones who make me who I am and together we create this thing called hope. I've called this book *The Church of Milk and Honey* because my experience with church, with

God, with hope, with love, is farther and wider than any book could contain. My church has been the nourishment you have generously given to me and to this life through your own bodies. My church has been the wonder and sweetness we have all made, together, without saying a word.

Take these words, now, from a few of my fellow travelers as nourishment for each week of the year and know that we are now connected, you and me and all of us, and allow that miracle to come through.

January Cinquain

Maria C. Goodson

Sun, Set:
the long first month,
Peaceful in its newness.
January: You can be you.
Moon, Rise.

January 2023

How to live

By Ann Quinn

Be kind, above all else.
But how to get ahead?
That one I only answer with another question:
Why? Who do you want to leave
behind? And do you really want
to be with those who've left the others
in the dust? If so,
I cannot help you. Life is hard.
I like it best down here
with people who are here to help.

I begin each morning by writing a few lines in iambic pentameter, also known as blank verse, in which the beats of the language thud along evenly like heartbeats. It's just an exercise, but sometimes something interesting comes out. I have re-lineated this, so there are no longer five beats per line, to make the message more clear.

6

By Amy Hoogs

ate in the afternoon, but too early to be considered evening, I sat in my apartment trying to decide whether or not to go for a run. I was living in downtown Honolulu, just off Waikiki and every moment of deliberation moved me closer to a run ending in less visibility and scenarios my best friend warned me against regularly. And I am not, by nature, a runner.

A return call from one of my favorites on the other coast of the Pacific Ocean interrupted my deliberations. We chatted for a moment and I mentioned my potential run. She asked which answer I wanted, and I replied, "Both."

"Okay," she offered, "you're young and healthy, and skipping one run to relax will not alter your life."

I leaned back and put my feet up, prompting her contrary advice.

As soon as the words left her mouth, I was up and reaching for the door, thanking her.

"Run. Because some people can't, and they want to."

In The Moment

By Loree Edwards

The older I get, the more life seems to pass by in a blur. Several years ago I read about the art of stopping and being in the moment. Literally stopping… on a hike, floating down a river, smelling that exquisite flower or just simply watching a sunset. While stopped, I began telling myself that this is a moment I wish to remember. I wanted to remember that wonderful feeling of being with loved ones, the amazing colors I was witnessing or being specific about whatever was special in this moment. I'm so glad I started this practice as I do have so many special memories in the forefront of my thoughts that would otherwise have been lost in that blur of time. Thanking your higher power for the gift of this moment finalizes these special moments. So easy of a practice, so monumental in results!

By Kathleen Van Velsor

My mother took me to the City that she loved in the early 1950's from the Peninsula that she also loved. Both had huge billowy fog banks but one had what she regarded as civility. The City was metropolitan and her goal that day was to show me some of the finer things.

So I was dressed in a hat, purse and crinoline with an indelicate sweater clip resembling two mink heads. The mink "hair" was exquisite but the clips kept coming loose. As I fidgeted I noticed my mother's shoes that showcased her toes, legs and a suit of gabardine.

We had driven to the Grey Hound bus station in Daly City, I think. Then we boarded a bus with a full load of passengers to a disembarking place very near the Emporium. I'll never forget this place. It was like a barn and had a certain smell of huge numbers of passengers. I couldn't wait to get into the open air on Market Street.

And where to next? Well since we were on a finery mission it had to be the elegant and exquisite City of Paris with its brilliant dome where I was allowed to experience the art of perfumery and the delicacy of coffee service with fine pastries. Hats in this French emporium were art forms. Dresses were "creations." Froth had nothing to do with lattes and everything to do with fine veils and shoulder wraps that were designed for opera goers who would glide into rotundas and balcony seats. This was old San Francisco—make no mistake—and Paris finery ran through its veins.

By the time it was noon we had a hunger alert. My mother steered the two of us to a downstairs/upstairs restaurant where English muffins were king. There I was to be instructed in the art of dining in Union Square. The food was of modest quality but the vibe was pure San Francisco Chronicle—reporters and columnists grabbing a bite to eat, or doing an interview. It was all Herb Caen columns on the table, racks of noisy cups, important people and the delicious perfection of buttered muffins and ham and poached eggs. Fresh squeezed orange juice was on the menu and dark English tea came in teapots and teacups.

My lessons started with how to use knives properly and when not to pick up an errant napkin off of the floor (the rule was, ahem, *never* pick it up). English muffins were to be coaxed open, never sliced. Butter bits were left to melt in their crevices while English jam lined the pockets.

Mother and I awkwardly made it through the first set of dining and visitor conventions. Then we were off, like cosmopolitan adventurers, to the Emporium!

By Carol Clupny

here is no excuse for forgetting my birthday. It's Valentine's Day! The tradition we now have of exchanging cards, giving flowers and sweets, and celebrating "love" started in the third century. Kind priests, living in different locations, yet all sharing the name Valentine, were attributed to encouraging good deeds. At one point someone must have said "Will the real Valentine please stand up?" The records do show a priest was beheaded for secretly performing marriages and saving many young men from going off to war. With only one documented Valentine, there wasn't enough evidence for validity. The name was taken off the catholic church's list of saints.

Yet the tradition of celebrating Valentine's Day continues.

As there were parties at school and events in the community my parents didn't always plan my birthday celebration. That doesn't mean there weren't some standouts throughout the years. I was traumatized by the Elks Club Father-Daughter dance. Growing up as a tomboy, the thought of shopping, choosing a dress and matching shoes, getting my hair cut and styled, and then actually dancing with my dad terrorized me. My fright was appeased by a buffet and in exchange for my misery I had a plateful of my favorite corn relish.

Like looking at a polaroid snapshot I have a cloudy memory of three of the five neighbor boys, their hair slicked back, and their white shirts buttoned up to the collar, sitting on the yellow bench where my brothers sat for dinner. Their faces showed their delight as my mom carried to the table a heart shaped cake with thick pink frosting and lit candles.

Later, Mom discovered heart-shaped cookie cutters. The cakes were replaced by sugar cookies with red frosting and tiny candy heart sprinkles. If I was traveling with the basketball team, she sent along a package that was meant to be shared. Somehow, they disappeared before my teammates got on the bus!

My sixteenth birthday was a bomb. My parents had a fight and dad left the house slamming the door. I stayed downstairs in my room listening to song dedications on the radio. When I finally dared to go upstairs, I saw an odd-shaped box, a small box of chocolates, flowers, and grocery store-baked valentine's cookies. The chocolate and flowers were for my mom. But in the box was an acoustic guitar and Dad remembered about the cookies.

I am far past the midpoint of my life. I have experienced many birthdays, and celebrations I do not remember.

Birthdays have an important place in marking the passage of time. Even if their numbers reflect my age. I can feel the years dragging behind me as they weigh me down. Those left ahead I can already tell are very much lighter.

I will continue to celebrate birthdays, with the few memories I have: the smiling neighbor boys, the candles on the cake, crumbs, and sprinkles left in the bottom of a plastic bag…and even the Father-Daughter dance.

These memories are my reward for having made it one more year. And those bits of candied sprinkles left in the bottom of the bag? They deserve an honorable mention for helping me enjoy the sweetness of my Valentine's Day birthday.

Patty Blank
By Patty Blank

Today is my birthday, February 22nd. On this day many years ago I was delivered on earth for yet another go at time and space. I picked this time, day and year to take my first breath knowing that this life would be full of adventure, change and challenges.

While I was in spirit "on the other side" my guides and angels collaborated with me in creating yet another journey to earth. We reviewed my past lives, dissecting each one, listing all the wins and losses, to imagine what I needed to accomplish this lifetime in order to get closer to God.

Each returning soul is required to develop a recipe to continue their evolution. The three main ingredients are how you will deal with everyday life, will you teach or learn and your overall energy.

The first component is the greatest. We have a choice of four; mental, emotional, physical and intuitive. I decided on physical. This life I thought "action" would allow me to grow more than the other three. If I keep moving I can master the others along the way. So far I have enjoyed living in 5 states in 35 homes, circumvented the world twice while touring over 80 countries, created 5 successful businesses and experienced true love 10 times. This life was meant to be a vacation!

Next I had to decide if I was going to be an extrovert or an introvert. This one took me a long time to decide. I finally raised my hand to be an ambivert. This time I wanted to enjoy both listening and talking. I wanted to learn and to teach. I wanted to think in solitude and express myself with words and movement.

The energy was also up in the air for me. Was I drawn to the male energy and independence, strength, power, growth and to be a leader? Or would I rather create, express myself, design a meaningful life to share with others and be part of a team with female energy? I have had so many lives as both. So this life I decided not to decide and went with both energies.

All souls design a foundation on which to grow for their next visit to earth. We understand we will be guided by our angels and also have freewill to make changes as we grow with each human life. Each soul has the same goal, that of evolution. We all plan to experience every possible lesson in order to gain wisdom to deal with whatever comes our way. As a soul we all want to be a God.

Remember we are not left out on our own during our time on earth. Metaphysics are available to all of us. At the age of 32 I was introduced to numerology. A friend gave me a complete chart of my current life. At first it scared me. How could it be that a complex number system knows all my inner thoughts and desires? However it verified that I had done everything with my life at that point to insure a happy life. Never again did I ever question my life decisions. I have always known I am on my designed path.

But wait, there is more. I used this life to master numerology. I have the ability to understand how my family, friends and lovers designed life paths. When I disagree with them I know why they do what they do and I accept them for who they are. Remember you can never change anyone. Once you realize this you too can lead a wise, fulfilled and happy life.

Leap Day

Maria C. Goodson

Once every four years, I am a day,
One dazzling day to stretch and leap.
What would you do, if your life was today?

Not sure what I am, when the day goes away:
it is dark, that I know: but I will not weep,
because once every four years, I am a DAY.

Will I let forth the sun, to shine on the bay?
Or take stock of myself, and do major upkeep?
What would you do, if your life was today?

Put on your shoes now, before time slips away:
today's not the day to stay wrapped in sleep.
Once every four years, I am a day.

I will buy myself an enormous bouquet,
and be kind to myself, like a friend I must keep.
What would you do, if your life was today?

Now is a portal, a shining pathway.
Wake up with panache and all I have to reap.
Once every four years, I am a day:
What will you do with your life today?

By Kara Panowitz

"Put yourself in the way of beauty" – from *Wild* by Cheryl Strayed "Awe is the salve that will heal our eyes" – Rumi

Awe. Not just happiness or curiosity, but downright eyes wide open, jaw dropping amazement. How have you experienced it? For me, it's nature: the purity in the color of flowers or the force of a crashing waterfall, standing among fall leaves swirling in the wind or walking through a valley of powerful mountains. Feeling awe is associated with happiness, lower stress levels, and a higher connection to yourself, others, and meaning of life. Seek awe fiercely. Hold it close to your heart and don't let anyone take its power from you. Call upon it when you need to breathe in time with the universe and fill every bit of your being with amazement.

Dragonflies (part I of VI)

By Jannica Cuaresma Breslin

Magdalene Street

Our house sits on Magdalene Street. The gate, the metal bars of the windows, and the roof are painted red. Flakes of rust sit on window sill and the earth around the house. I like that it has a little bit of color, because the rest of the house is gray. Different shades of gray, but gray nonetheless. Well, not the door to the house. It's dark brown. It's made of wood that's so big and heavy, it's kind of hard to open. It's hard to open with my little hands.

My mom and I are outside of the gate, waiting for the bus. My mom is holding my hand, because she doesn't want me to run around and play. She doesn't like it when I sweat through my clothes. She doesn't like it when I get dirt on my clothes. She doesn't like it when I get tired. She doesn't like it when I go too far down either side of the street. She doesn't like it when I go to the neighbors' houses and play with the other kids. She doesn't like it when I ask why.

So I watch the dragonflies. There are some, a dozen I think, hovering near the gate, hovering above the flowering weeds that somehow found their way through the cement ground and to the world outside. Their colors come out so nice in the sunlight. Some are light blue like the sky on a nice day. Some are dark blue like the sky when rain is about to come. Some are pink like the floor at my aunt's house, where my mom gets her hair permed. Some are yellow like my pencil. And some even have different colors on their skin and wings. I bet they fly all over the world to find all kinds of flowering weeds that they like.

Sometimes, I dream that I can fly.

I want to take my black leather shoes off. They're so hard. They're making the backs of my feet sting. Last time I wore them, I got blisters exactly where they're stinging now. But, if I go to school without shoes, the teacher will get mad at me. All of the girls are supposed to wear a white button shirt that is tucked into a long blue skirt, white socks with laces fluttering at the top, and black leather shoes. Those are the rules, and everyone has to follow the rules. And if I come home with dirty feet later, my mom will get mad at me and scold me. I might even get the belt.

I don't want to get the belt.

I guess I won't take my shoes off.

The bus arrives, my mom kisses me goodbye, and I get in, pretending my feet don't hurt.

Dragonflies (part II of VI)

By Jannica Cuaresma Breslin

1st Grade

The bus ride to school is always awful. No matter how far I stick my head out of the window to catch air, I always end up getting sick. At least I've learned to throw up outside of the window instead of on myself, and the other kids have stopped making fun of me.

Once we arrive, we drop our backpacks off at our classrooms and line up by classes on the field. There are no arms or feet out of place. Everyone s facing the cement stage. Our right hands rise to our chests and we sing the national anthem. There's a boy on the stage leading the song on the standing microphone. I wonder how early his bus had come and how fast he had run past everyone else who wanted to lead the anthem today. Lots of boys want to lead the anthem. Sometimes, I want to, too.

We walk back to our class without breaking our lines. There are flowering weeds near my classroom's door. I count three dragonflies. They are chasing each other. But, they fly away when we get close.

The solar system is drawn on the chalkboard. The nine planets are stuck on their orbits. The sun is like an egg yolk in the middle of it all. I imagine poking it until its yellow insides drip down.

There's a girl at the front of the class describing what Venus is like. I'm having a hard time listening, because I'm trying really hard to hold my pee until lunch recess. I don't like going to the bathroom during class because everyone will see. Everyone will watch. Everyone in class will see you leave. Everyone in the other classes will watch you pass by. And it's the same when you go back. I feel a little pain underneath my belly button, but I tell it to go hang in there. Just a little longer.

In time, the teacher dismisses us, and I get through the rest of the day just fine. I'm always just fine.

Dragonflies (part III of VI)

By Jannica Cuaresma Breslin

The Driver

My mom told me I won't ride the bus anymore. I don't remember if I didn't hear her tell me why, or if she didn't. It doesn't matter. I just won't ride the bus anymore. Instead, the old man who lives at the end of the street will drive me to and from school. He's my friend's dad. Well, I don't play with my friend anymore. I'm not supposed to. I think her cousin used to date my baby brother's nanny. They had a bad break up. I think that's why I'm not allowed to play with my friend.

The old man drives up to the front of our house, and so my mom kisses me goodbye. I look to the flowering weeds near the gate. There are only a few dragonflies flying around today. Someone must've caught a bunch of them yesterday. People like to catch dragonflies in small plastic bags, and they keep them inside. They are protected inside, until they die.

I get in the car. The old man is friendly. He has red cheeks. He smiles at me, but doesn't talk to me at all. He drives. The windows are open, and the wind feels cold on my face. It's not stuffy like the bus. I don't feel any rumbling in my tummy, and I start to enjoy the ride, and I imagine I can fly.

Dragonflies (part IV of VI)
By Jannica Cuaresma Breslin

The Bathroom

The boy at the front is describing Mars, and I'm having a hard time listening again. I can't hold my pee much longer. Maybe because I didn't throw up earlier, I'm all full inside. So I raise my hand. The teacher comes. Her black leather shoes must be harder than mine because they make a lot of noise on the floor. Tap tap tap tap tap. I ask for her permission to use the bathroom. I put my hands on my skirt to show her how desperate I am. She allows me to go, but reminds me to hurry so I don't miss too much of the lesson on Mars. I nod my head, even though I don't care about Mars. I don't understand why we're learning about places we will never go to.

I jump out of my chair and march right out. I almost trip over my rolling bag, but I keep my head up and eyes on the door. When I get outside, I march faster and keep my eyes on the opening at the end of the building. I pass four classrooms without looking away from the bathroom. I even forget to look for dragonflies. The pee is almost out. The pain underneath my belly button has awoken. I rush past the janitor who is sweeping right outside of the bathrooms. I make it to the very first stall and take a long breath out as I pee.

The whole bathroom is covered with blue tiles the size of my palms. There are two sinks near the door, and three stalls against the wall. The stalls are pretty long, probably to make up for the fact that they didn't have doors. I look at the tiles around my feet, covered with a little glimmer of black from my shoes.

Oddly enough, the rest of my stall gets dark. I see something move in the tiles in front of me, and I realize that that moving shadow is in every tile all around me. After a few seconds, the shadow stops moving. It is still, and much bigger now. I look up. The janitor stands at the opening of my stall. He is looking up and down. His eyes are intent, like he is wondering what I am doing. I don't understand why he doesn't understand. I don't understand why he's there.

He takes a few steps towards me, a broom in one hand.

He is blocking sunlight from reaching my stall.

I jump at the sound of the broom dropping beside me.

I stand as fast as I can, and pull my panties up as fast as I can. But my heart is crawling out of my throat, and I don't know which way is out. There is no out. He is right in front of me. His shadow has swallowed all the light.

He reaches out behind me, and I feel his rough skin squeezing through the garter of my skirt. I feel more hands behind me. The shadows are also touching me.

All of the hands are hot, like the face of an iron when the dial is turned all the way to the right. All of the hands are burning me. The pain underneath my belly button is back and is all over my body. The tiles are spinning and closing in. I want to break free of the searing pain.

I am being punished, but I don't know what I did.

This is wrong.

I am in something wrong.

I am going to get into so much trouble.

I am going to get the belt.

I don't want to get the belt, so I push.

I push again.

And again.

And I fall.

For a few seconds, I don't feel the hot hands and I force myself to crawl. My elbows and shoes are slipping against the blackened tiles. It's hard to move my legs with my clothes all messed up.

I feel the hot hands on my back, and I push further with all my might. My left shoe comes off. I am crawling up on the wall, but falling on my knees. I feel the hot hands tug my hair, and I pull away with my left foot.

And I run.

I can hear the janitor calling me back, but I keep running with my eyes towards my classroom.

I run like I've never ever run before in my life.

I run, and I fall onto my chair, which is wet and squishy. I guess I peed on myself, but I don't know when I did.

I look around, trying to remember where I am.

I am at school.

The boy is talking about Mars.

I…

I see shadows on blue tiles. I feel hot hands around me.

I feel dirty.

I am dirty.

I look to my right and see the girl who went to the bathroom before me. I ask her if something happened to her in the bathroom. She said she doesn't want to talk about it.

I guess I don't want to talk about it either.

$\mathcal{Dragonflies}$ (part V of VI)

By Jannica Cuaresma Breslin

The Stranger

After school, I go to the bench right outside of the school gate. The old man told me to wait there for him. But I went to the back of the school and all the way around the building, away from the bathrooms. I drag my rolling bag close behind me to cover my wet butt.

I'm glad I don't have to go into the school bus. They will all make fun of me again. "Ew, who smells like the toilet?" "Look, it's shi shi girl!" "Gross! She's covered in germs!" "She doesn't know how to use the bathroom or clean herself!" They won't even bother whispering. And they will all laugh.

I sit on the bench. The grass along the street are dry. No flowering weeds. No dragonflies. I can't blame them. I am sticky all over underneath my skirt. The smell of pee is swirling all over me. I wouldn't want to hang around me either.

The sky is a little more orange now and the sun is hanging low. The old man is still not here. Maybe I missed him because I took so long walking around the school. There is light buzzing and whistling in the dead and dying grasses. I guess the nighttime insects are waking up.

The wind is getting colder, but my face is still hot. Not my whole face. Just where the tears are coming down.

A car passes by. So many cars have passed by. But this one stops, slowly drives backwards, then stops again in front of me. The man gets out of the car and stands by his car. I try to look at him, but there's so much tears in my eyes and I can't see him clearly. I can see him looking around. I don't know what he's looking for. The school is closed. All the buses are gone. Everyone else has been picked up. There is nothing to find.

He asks me a lot of questions. Why am I out here alone? Why didn't I ride the bus? Where are my parents? Who is supposed to pick me up? Why am I crying? Oddly, he doesn't ask about the smell.

I want to answer, but I am too tired to do anything else but cry.

The man walks down the street, his head turning in all directions. He walks down the street the other way. He looks confused. He sounds like he might cry, too.

He asks me more questions. Where do I live? What city? What town? What district?

I tell him my address. I memorized it a long time ago. I tell him my house is red and there are dragonflies outside.

He shakes his hands at the sky.

He asks me more questions. What is near my house? Any big buildings? Any store?

I tell him there's a farm near one end of the street. That's where all the frogs come from. At the other end of the street, my friend's family has a store. I like to buy bubblegum from there. There's a church with a big field and one see-saw a few streets away. And somewhere, but I don't know where, there's a river. There's a boat that you can ride, and the boat man pulls a string so you can cross the river.

I stop. I cry harder, because even if I know where I am now and I know where I want to be, I realize I am lost.

I am dirty.

I am lost.

I am ashamed.

I hug my knees, and scoop up my skirt. I bury my face in it, even though it reeks.

The man kneels in front of me. He says he can try to take me home if I'm ok with it. Or we can call the police and wait.

I shake my head. I don't want to go to jail.

I am dirty.

I am lost.

I am ashamed.

The sky is a little purple now. It'll be black soon. Maybe in an hour.

I don't think the old man is coming at all, and so I mumble a yes and walk towards the man. His hands gently pat my shoulders. They don't burn like the janitor's.

The man seems afraid of me. Of me? He's much bigger than I am. Why is he afraid of me? What would I do to him? Or maybe he's not afraid of me. But, he's afraid of something.

As he drives, he points things out on the road, and asks if I recognize them. I tell him no, and he tells me it's ok. He doesn't get tired of not getting the answers he wants. He just keeps asking his questions.

Finally, I recognize the hardware store that's one street over from my street. I tell the man where to go from there.

The man stops his car at our red gate. He asks if I'm sure if I live here, and I tell him yes. He still has fear in his eyes, but he tells me to go home. I get out of the car and open the gate. I look back and see smoke come out of the back of the car as it drives away.

I didn't get to say thank you.

34

Dragonflies (part VI of VI)
By Jannica Cuaresma Breslin

Good People

My mom isn't home. I'm sure she's mad at me, and I don't want to make her more mad by hiding from her. So I put my things down behind the wooden door, and then go outside again. I sit on the little cement step in front of our gate.

I see my mom walking up from one end of the street. She sees me, and runs. She grabs me. Lifts my arms. Turns me around. Feels like my legs. Combs through my hair. Cups my cheeks. Hugs me tight. Tighter than she's ever done, but somehow softer than she's ever done. I want to say sorry, but I am too ashamed to say anything.

Inside, we sit down facing each other, the way we always sit when I have to tell the truth. I tell my mom what happened, even the parts that I don't understand or know how to explain. She pulls me in her arms again. She is rocking me back and forth, and I close my eyes. I feel warm inside her hug, like when you're wrapped in a blanket while there's a storm outside.

My mom and I are our way to school, and she tells me that the old man got drunk and forgot to pick me up, and she left to get me as soon as she found out. When she got there and no one was there, she felt like she was going to die. But, it doesn't matter. The old man won't be driving me anywhere anymore. And we are only going to that school just one more time.

When we get there, I bury my head into my mom's shirt so that the janitor won't see me, wherever he was. And better yet, I won't see him, wherever he was. I think my mom knows what I'm trying to do. She puts her arm around my head to bury it, too.

We make our way to the office and sit in front of the principal's desk. As my mom talks, the principal nods her head. I see that she can hear my mom, but she isn't listening. She tells my mom that I must've misunderstood what happened. She knows the janitor. She says he's a good man.

My mom slams her hand on the desk, stands up, and drags me out. I grab at her. I want to bury my face in her shirt again, but she stops us both. She pulls my head up. She straightens her body, and pulls my weight up so that I stand up straight, like her. We walk out of the school hand-in-hand without looking back.

I see a dragonfly pass by in front of me as we close the school gate. Just one. It is green like a shiny new leaf. I wonder where it's going.

Intimacy and Accountability: finding peace with myself and others

By Giuse Varni

Recently I went to a retreat with dear friends. After a night of me sharing and presenting, and others sharing in response, I was triggered. I perceived others were criticizing what specific language and materials I chose to use. In the next morning, these thoughts arose from our group silent meditation:

In this moment I feel confused about why/how this time with wonderful women would bring up feeling like I'm wrong for using certain phrases; like now I must watch what I say, or people will think I'm not being kind to myself. When, in the beginning of the retreat I was being kind to myself in choosing what I chose.

In this moment I see friends, flawed people, perfect humans; people I want to get along with, love, and be loved by. People just trying to put their own stuff in order and navigate through life.

In this moment I see distance/ a gap.

In this moment I feel angry at people for making me feel like my shares are inadequate. When they are trying to talk about complete acceptance. So, what is this Higher Power? What is the defect? Thinking others can make me feel anything?

In this moment I notice that I want to be loved. I notice I do love myself. I notice probably others want to be loving. I am true to myself. I am kind to myself. This I have learned in the rooms with others, and through my Higher Power.

In this moment I am aware of my hurt and humanness. I am aware I can only bring what resonates with me. I can be ok with what resonates with myself. I can be ok with my whole self.

Be here now… breath here now.

I realize I can let my friends be exactly where they are and appreciate what they share and know. For, even if, like me, they don't know everything or do everything perfectly; they do a lot well, and have a lot of goodness that I can and do benefit from regularly.

Olive's Birth

By Kristie Graybill

Birth has the tendency to unveil your greatest fears and expose areas of strength that you never knew existed. For me, this third baby has freed my soul and changed me in ways I'm not quite able to put into words. But before the days of toddler messes and newborn cuddles cloud my memory, I must put my best foot forward in jotting down the details of this triumphant day. The day our Olive June arrived.

Our home birth story came at the start of a new decade. Quite literally, too, as Olive made her grand entrance earth side twelve days after the new year. A due date babe. A baby born after 29 hours of physical, emotional and spiritual turmoil. 29 hours of facing my physical fears and pleading with God to remove the pain and to offer supernatural strength. Strength I knew I could not muster up in my own doing. 29 hours of trusting the process. Trusting my body to do what it was born to do. After 29 hours, light transcended the darkness and my daughter was in my arms.

This was my third pregnancy in four years. The first two were beautiful, unmedicated hospital births that I was fortunate enough to have no complications pre or postnatally. Both of which I felt supported, heard and validated in all my birthing requests. However, with the switch from healthcare insurance companies, doors opened for our family to pursue my desire for a home birth. To us, our home is sacred. A space we moved into as newlyweds. Our first big purchase together as a married couple. A space that allowed us to begin our family of three and then soon after our party of four. With the plan to move within the year, we could think of no better way but to celebrate the birth of our third child within the walls that already held so much love and memories and togetherness.

While the name we chose for her was a nod to the peaceful olive branch, the labor she and I wrestled through couldn't be further from this. Right away, contractions were close together and filled with intensity. The birth team gathered shortly after I contacted them and the house soon filled with feelings of anticipation and excitement. A baby was soon being born into the world! Who could think of a better way to spend the weekend?!? The clock ticked and labor progressed, slowly but surely. The birth team patient, kind and plenty encouraging. My husband, my dear husband, working tirelessly to get the hose attached so I could labor in the tub.

The tub was filled and located in the center of our bedroom. A symbol of tranquility. During intense contractions, I wanted to be nowhere else except in the water. Unfortunately, though, the water slowed my labor down drastically and even stopped contractions all together. This prompted my team to encourage me to get moving. Lunges, squats, stairs. Dilation was slow, tumultuous and incredibly painful. My midwife and her attendant thought the unpredictable labor pattern I was experiencing was due to Olive's positioning in the womb. My doula and best friend, educated in Spinning Babies and other positioning exercises, thought it best to use asymmetrical movements which would help Olive descend into the pelvis. After laboring for close to 20 hours, the team needed a little rest. The labor gods were kind to both Olive and I as the intensity paused for a few hours and Tyler and I were able to get some rest. Our birth workers snoozed on the floor of my daughters' room.

Around 5:15 am the next day, I texted them for my (and Olive's) vitals to be checked. Both of which came back normal. While my family and friends were wondering where this baby was and what was the hold up, my team remained calm and assured both Tyler and I that time was the only thing this babe needed to emerge. And more movement and exercise. I pleaded desperately with them to let me just get back into the tub. They heard my request but explained that draining and refilling (since the water was cold and at risk of containing bacteria at this point) would take an hour or more. My midwife gave me a peanut ball and I laid on the bed to labor there while the tub refilled. My contractions became incredibly intense and my laboring sounds changed. Both Tyler and the attendant were downstairs heating up pots of water on the stove to hurry the tub filling process along. I felt the urge to push powerfully and deeply and Olive's head appeared! The midwife yelled that the head was born and they hurried upstairs. Three strong pushes later and a midwife's hand assisting Olive's shoulders in sliding out, she plopped on my bed. Stunned, I stared at my crying baby. Tyler announced the gender and I slowly repositioned so I could hold her on my chest. All the pain was gone. Never to be felt again. The contractions vanished. The vomiting subsided. The uncontrollable shaking disappeared. Never did I think this moment would emerge but as with all suffering and pain, dawn eventually emerges. A beautiful birth story etched in my memory and never to be physically, emotionally and spiritually felt again.

While, in the moment, I wanted nothing more than relief and for it all to be over, I do not regret a single decision I made leading up to her entrance into the world. I had to experience the pain of January 11th to gain the joy of January 12th.

Welcome to the world, sweet girl.

Lessons I Have Learned From The Trees

By Gina Strauss

Our roots are all connected.
If you are an Oak seed, don't try to be a Maple tree.
It is okay to let go of old "leaves" when the time is right.
Turn towards what supports your growth.
The Dwarf Willow is just as special as the Giant Sequoia.
If you have strong roots, it is easier to bend with the wind.
We are majestic in every season of our lives.

By Marylou Fusco

*Y*ears ago I was attacked by mockingbirds every time I left my house. They had built their nest in our neighbors' shrubbery and at some point I had gotten too close. I never even saw the nest, but the birds saw me. They remembered. Ironically my neighbors and housemates escaped their outrage. Every morning my housemates would watch, stifling laughter, as I ran onto the sidewalk with my arms protecting my head. It got so bad that I took to wearing my bicycle helmet whenever I left the house. After a while the attacks stopped. The chicks had hatched or the mockingbirds no longer saw me as a threat.

I was a country kid who tolerated or was indifferent to nature. Now I've lived in cities for so long I expect nature to be contained or, at least, out of sight. I'm annoyed when other creatures intrude on my spaces. Birds are not supposed to dive-bomb your head. Mice race through our walls every winter. When we find spiders in our basement my small daughter begs me to kill them. I lecture her on acceptance and the realities of city living while secretly plotting the most efficient methods of removal. I have my own nest to protect.

These days I live next to a park in a different city. Each year the park attracts hundreds of migratory birds. When I go for walks I try to identify their different coloring or calls. Sometimes I'm so wrapped up in my own thoughts that I forget to look around me. These birds probably see and assess me although nothing like the urgency of ones protecting their nest. For the birds, the park is a temporary stopover, and I am neither predator nor prey. I am a creature like them or maybe one more akin to tree or pond. An ordinary human walking through our shared, hallowed ground.

Julius Sings

By Nicole Shea

Let this day be this day
Pleasant
Tragic
Productive
Forgettable
The mass of forgettable minutes bubbles
Pulsingly alive forming mycelium threads with, for example, time
    spent by a river.
Mount Tom rises where Connecticut flows.
At the river's edge, dinosaurs, and modern girls.
Julius sang *Wade in the Water*.
A day—floating along a stream.
A day—submerged by a flood.
A day—dragged from the river, saved by another soul's breath, or
    God's will.
God's gonna trouble the waters.
Wade in.

In memory of Julius Lester 1939 – 2018

Week 22

By Galen Peterson

The first hints of dawn will begin in another thirty minutes. It is perfect. By the time I'm washed up for the day and the coffee brewed, it will be ready.

The steam of the coffee warms my face and the brilliant hues of a new day rising warms my soul. As the undersides of clouds glow, worries melt away. In the face of such stark beauty and grandness, my small role in this magnificent bigger world is put into perspective. There is comfort in having a tiny place in the big picture, and joy in not knowing where it will lead. I am no Altas and if I must shrug, life will go on. Thank God.

The soft light and strong taste of the coffee remind me of my purpose on this walk through life. I've seen that softness in another's eye and felt the strength of friendship. Today I will soak in the joy of the sunrise so I can share it with my family and my friends. There is amazing beauty in putting a smile on another's face. Investing the time and energy to tell another they are important and loved provides inner strength to both.

We are the coffee and light of the coming day for those experiencing a cloudy season. Storms crash on the soul, darkening the way and soaking the weary traveler. The new day forming gives hope to continue. Most of the time, we don't even know the impact we have on others, and that is the beauty of being the sunrise.

When the cup runs empty, no worries. The sunset will come soon, and it will be spectacular. The smoke and dust of the day allow the sun to burst from the mountain horizon in glory. In grace, the light will slowly transform the whole sky and my cup will flow over.

Tomorrow morning, we shall renew once more.

Beautiful Kisses
By Jannica Cuaresma Breslin

Mutual one night stand -
Short-lived physical electricity, shared between two
Long-lived memory of spontaneity crawling from the skin to the lips

End of a long and impersonal acquaintance -
End of passersby gazes and grazes
End of almost coincidences
End of group rates and
Respondez s'il vous plait
End of hit and miss

Trial and error and happy shrugs -
Equal exertion of effort
Equal exercise of forgiveness
Equal exhaustion of try-agains
Sincere handshakes between pacifists

Bitter-sweet goodbye and gratitude -
Minds, bodies, emotions, and souls
Bent and stretched to their fullest extent,
But circumstances outweighing them all
Still, a battle lost is a war won,
So long as the fight against the circumstances
Is appreciated for its spirit and intent

Best friends blossoming, finally -
Fear of crossing boundaries,
Fear of submitting one's heart
To the one who knows it best
And having it returned to you before
It leaves your hand,
And fear of breaking what wasn't broken
All conquered,
Because there are more things to trust,
Look forward to, discover,
Share, celebrate, and nurture

Leap of faith landing gracefully -
Digging for signals
Grows up to accepting
The unpredictability of the weather
In a seemingly steady climate,
To planting a new seed,
To watering with a smile of hope,
And to enjoying the sprouting relationship

Water Reflection

By Rosanne Shank

I walk to a nearby place with countless smooth round rocks. The rocks move in and out with the tide, singing songs all day long. The gentle tumbling is a calm encouragement and I sense that the ocean has been waiting for me.

I dip my toes and then little by little the rest of me slides in, effortlessly.

I am wrapped in a loving hold,
the one that lets me be me,
Here and now.
The only things that matter
Are around me,
Every inch of me.
And it feels wonderful.
I feel like I belong.
I feel joy.
I feel light.
Like I am loved,
Like I am the most important thing; the only thing…

Benediction

By Kristen Zory King

y body cuts through the dark in a chaotic rhythm. I am breathing hard, sweat slick across my arms, chest, back, face, legs. A soft breeze enters the room and for a brief moment, there is a flash of mercy before me—more feeling than intellect, a reflex thread through muscle and burrowed deep in bone, long known but forgotten—as the wind relieves each limb from the heat it has generated through movement. It is after a year of deep grieving that I find myself here: blindfolded alongside strangers from around the world and taking part in a synchronized breathing ceremony to recalibrate and reconnect with my central nervous system. We are in Costa Rica, about half a mile from the Pacific Ocean, all of us in search of something, some part of ourselves, that we've seemed to misplace. We've traveled by car and bus and plane, far and wide, driven forward by what we seek, following a map faded and folded and placed neatly beside our hearts.

Breath and air filter through our bodies at an alternating pace—sometimes shallow, sometimes deep, sometimes harsh, sometimes slow—as we follow the instructions given to us. Move your body. Don't stop. Breath. Deeper. Give in to what arises within you. Give in to your breath. Give in to your body. Give in to your movement. Give in to yourself. Around me I hear monkeys screaming, geckos chirping, people breathing, grunting, crying, laughing. I am surprised to find some of these sounds rising from my own throat, tears mixed with sweat pouring from my own eyes. In the safety of the darkness, of the jungle, of this room loud and vibrating from the sounds and sweat and movement all around me, I, too, scream. I, too, laugh. I, too, cry. I, too, give in.

When it is over, I am led, still blindfolded, to sit by another, my hands placed in theirs. I think, by the roughness and size, they are the hands of a man and I feel another flash of warmth and grace as hope rises within me that I am partnered with A, with whom I've shared a friendship both gentle and kind over the last two weeks of our yoga teacher training program. But my hands are smaller than most and I divorce myself from the attachment that comes with hope, the wish that these hands belong to one person or another. Hope, I've learned, is a feeling that lives in the future. And the future, I know, is fickle. What I can trust is this moment, each second unfolding simply before me at its own pace, its own rhythm. So I allow instead the immediate, the present, the now, my hands holding another's in silence, exhaustion, an understanding both ancient and animal.

When the blindfolds are removed, I see the blue of A's eyes and smile. I was right. It was him, my sweet friend, brother of five, teacher, leader, husband, friend. I feel, in this moment, a love not unlike the mercy of the wind, the grace of hope. It is not romantic. Not even platonic. It is something deeper, bigger, simpler, known, true. I remove my hands from A's and place them over my heart, feeling the symmetry of each hard beat beneath my palms. I am, at once, connected to A, to the world around me, and to the world within. Here, 3,500 miles from my home, riddled with mosquito bites, muscles and mind sore from days and hours of yoga, meditation, learning and unlearning, I understand the totality of connection, of love, of the Divine. I find, in a moment that stretches both seconds and lifetimes, the part of myself I had been seeking, hear the laughter around me as others discover the same. What we lost, it seems, never strayed all that far away. It was right here, beating strong and fast in our chests. All we needed was a little help finding it. All we needed was the tender touch of a friend's hand.

58

Of Time and Space
By Nancy Carver Wade

Many years ago, my husband and I traveled to the east coast to visit the Situate, Massachusetts area, the former home of his paternal grandparents. While we were there, we visited the Plimouth Paxtuxet Museums in Plymouth, an authentic 17th century village designed to duplicate the first Plymouth plantation. During our visit, we encountered several inhabitants, played by local actors, who very realistically played the parts of villagers, merchants, and craftsmen and women. My maiden name is Carver and at one point, my husband asked one of the citizen actors if he knew John Carver, the first governor of the Plymouth Colony. "Oh yes," the man replied with a strong British accent. "He died in the cornfield. Clutched his chest and just fell over. Terrible thing it was. Just terrible." We were drawn into the scene, feeling a bit like history was unfolding before us.

My husband enjoyed genealogy, as did my Mom, who was in her 60's at the time. I was not as enthralled. To me, this kind of research seemed like a tedious task, a search for names and historical dates that went back in time but had little to do with me.

But a few years ago, I began thinking about the many stories I heard growing up: stories about my Dad's family, tragic stories of untimely deaths and financial ruin. I remembered hearing that my great grandfather had been shot and killed during a home burglary, that a few years prior, three of his young grandsons had died in accidents, and how, 20 years later, his youngest son would be convicted of extortion and sent to federal prison. I wondered what I might be able to find online about these relatives of mine, ancestors whom I never knew.

Since that recollection, I have immersed myself in researching one small branch of my Dad's family tree: my great-grandfather, his first wife (who died in childbirth on Christmas Day 1893) and his second wife, sister of the first, whom he married a few years later. I have learned all that I can about this couple and the five children they raised to adulthood.

The youngest son, in particular, has captured my attention and my imagination. Raymond was raised in southern Colorado and in the ski town of Steamboat Springs. He was sent to prep school in Boulder, where I now live. I have uncovered photos of him as a high school baseball player and as a pitcher in the minor leagues in Texas. I have stood in front of the boarding house near the University of Colorado where he and his brother, Lewis, shared a room.

I have unearthed original court pleadings from the national archives and his complete inmate file from Leavenworth Prison in Kansas. Each factoid and file propel me onward; I want to learn more and more. I have been amazed by the treasure trove of material available and by the generosity of fellow researchers and archivists.

Raymond has come to life in my mind and in my heart; I feel strangely protective of him. As I uncover facts, dates, and geographical locations related to this family, I look forward to breathing life into their stories and using my imagination to wonder about days gone by.

Week 27

Anonymous

"You will know when it is time to leave". That is what my Al-Anon sponsor said to me after our homegroup meeting one night. I was confused.

I knew what she meant but I was not aware that I had shared about needing or wanting to leave anyone or anything. I knew what she meant, if I continued to practice recovery: reading Al-Anon literature; making time for prayer and meditation; listening, and sharing my experience, strength and hope I would know when it was time to take appropriate action. Her words stayed with me as a beacon in a shifting landscape that could be obscured by fog.

Over the next few years, I made a number of rather dramatic changes in my life, one at a time and each led me to the next change. None came "out of nowhere," though it might have seemed that way to my friends and family, but were the result of paying attention to where I was at a given moment and knowing that I only had to do what was needed in that moment. Sometimes, that simply meant taking care of basic needs (food, water, brushing my teeth, taking a hot shower), at other times it meant doing something enjoyable and recognizing what I enjoyed and at other times it meant making a difficult phone call, scheduling an appointment or doing further research to explore my options. Through all of those moments, I tried to pay attention to what I was doing and take time to listen to my body, my heart, my mind and emotions.

As is so often stated, change is inevitable, pain is inevitable but suffering does not have to go on indefinitely. I am growing and changing each day that I am alive and I can choose to grow stronger; if not physically, I can grow in understanding, courage, awareness, courage and confidence by growing my recovery practice in this moment.

Musings on my birthday!

By Sonia Martinez

I have reached, and passed, many milestones...and am now in the upper half of my 80s. I am usually amused when I hear young 20 and 30 somethings talk about aging and dreading birthdays. I once read an essay where the author wrote: 'We see the pretty 25 year-olds and sigh. But, we were once also 25, just like they will one day be our age.'...and I add, if they're lucky to live this long. Today I am 87 years old and feel blessed to wake up every morning and greet the day...wondering what each will bring and enjoying each to the fullest... I love the younger ones their zest for life, but I keep on keeping on...and there is still zest of a different kind in mine. I have never dreaded birthdays...or felt any anxiety over getting older. Each birthday is a milestone and an achievement...as long as I'm here to celebrate them...bring them on! Of course, there are things I miss about being young...like the ability and stamina to get around more, hike, run, garden as I used to are just a few of them....but there are other compensations, and the reality of having lived, having done, having achieved, having loved...(however misguided) ...all of that, no one can take away from me. The alternative to not losing our 'youth' is to die young...and I prefer to grow old...to wake up and greet every morning for as long as I can...and anyway...isn't youth wasted on the young? It might be just a trite saying, but when you think about it...we all wasted much of our youth on unimportant things..

I remember my Daddy laughing

By Joan van Velsor

My childhood was extraordinarily blessed. Our finances were quite modest, but I had the great good fortune to have parents who loved each other, and a good humored father who found happiness in an ordinary life.

Henry Stanley Abbott grew up on a wheat farm in Kansas, homesteaded by his grandparents. He graduated with a degree in Math from a small religious college in southern California. World War II and the US Army brought him to San Francisco, where he married my mother and lived the rest of his life.

Intending to teach mathematics, the shortage of jobs following World War II meant he worked instead as a skilled tradesman in a physically demanding, blue collar job. This must have been deeply disappointing; he had planned for a life centered on learning, with thoughtful colleagues, and serious students. We never saw this disappointment, but he took serious interest in our studies, teaching me to read before I went to Kindergarten, encouraging experiments in electricity and science, and making sure we had our own Encyclopedia Britannica on the shelf on a pay-by-the-month schedule.

Deeply religious, he was a member of a fundamentalist church, serving in various board positions, as Sunday School teacher and as counselor. My parents tithed at least 10% of their gross income all of their lives. The church, and the members of it's congregation, were the center of our lives. My parents grew up in an age when their contemporaries aspired to "higher things." They aspired to serve noble causes, to live honorably, to have their word be more dependable than any written contract. These were the values they taught, and lived.

My father left no wealth, no widespread fame, no record of extraordinary achievements. But the memory of his choice to be happy, to find joy in his life as it was, and to insure that his family knew they were loved, provided a secure foundation for myself and my two siblings. And he laughed. He could cheer us up when we had one of those minor childhood vomiting episodes. He would invariably say "Hasten Jason, bring the basin. Oops too late, bring the mop." Silly, but it made us smile.

My father died at age 47 from a stroke, a devastating event for his family. I am profoundly grateful for the 14 years I had as his daughter. They gave me a lasting feeling of worthiness, values to live up to, and an unwavering belief in the essential joy and goodness of life. No child can ask for more.

eve

By Kristen Zory King

never have i come closer to god
than in july my body a garden
nightshade plump mosquito tender
humid and flush taut between
earth and open sky and oh! should
i be reborn may it be as tomato
round in rough hand what could be
more human what could be more
divine than my skin summer warm
soil stained my juices ripe and
sweet dripping from his chin

No-Matter-What Love

By Emily J. Telfair Hadley

It was the last evening of summer vacation with my family. The sun was setting and we had just reeled in the kite from its last flight of the season. Everyone else was walking back to the house and I had a few moments alone with my five year old nephew. All week I had been waiting for a moment to teach him one of those precious life lessons a godparent is privileged to pass along to a godchild. I wanted to teach him about *unconditional love.*

Jackson, I'm going to teach you a new word, "unconditional." Do you know what this word means? No, he replied. It means that there is a special kind of love that your mom and dad and your meemaw and poppy and your Uncle Chris and I all have for you. It means that we are going to love you no matter what. Do you know how God loves all people even when they do good things and not so good things? Oh yeah, God loves everybody, even the bad guys. Yes, so all of your family, we are going to love you like God loves you and you can love yourself that way too. *This is unconditional love.*

We all have an inner five year old who may welcome a reminder of what has always been true: that we deserve to be here and that we are worthy of love that we never had to earn.

And if this is a message that was not spelled out to you this clearly at another stage of your life, then I offer it to you now:

This I promise you, dear one, you are loved – no matter what.

Prayer for Jean Allen
By Jan Woodcock

Tell me, God
how it really is at the gates.

Surely, it will be a surprise
when all the theologians who write those esoteric religious treatises
with all the ontological, exegetical explanations
find themselves moving over —
moving over for the quiet and faithful ones . . .

Surely, it will be a surprise
when the ones who taught all the classes
find themselves moving over
for the mothers, for the gardeners,
for the ones who plant the trees and the flowers,
and who bring the raspberries in.

Surely, the wisdom writers will find themselves
moving over for the ones who live out Your Wisdom'
who do the loving things,
who welcome the newcomers,
and who offer kind words.

Surely, at the gates the ones with all the answers will find themselves
moving over for the ones with the gentle questions,
for the peacemakers,
for those with the helping hands,
for those who sit in the nursery with the children on their laps –
the children who are too young to know
that this fine person who holds them
held us all
in her just and loving ways,
with her encouraging words,
with her fine mind,
with the truth and integrity of her spirit.

So, Dear God, however it all goes up there, or out there, or in here,
maybe it will go a little better now.
You've got the best and the brightest now,
the most loving, and the most just.
We had her too,
and we are truly grateful.

Thank you, God.
And thank you, Auntie

Amen

September 15, 1992

Redefining Failure

By Siobhan McKenna

> "Life is made up of moments,
> small pieces of glittering mica
> in a long stretch of gray cement."
>
> -Anna Quindlen

One summer in my twenties, I traveled to Anchorage jobless on a whim. I didn't have any close friends or family who lived there, but the fantasy of a place that moved slower and in-tune with nature called to me.

In the city, I found a part-time job and set out to explore. I hiked in the Chugach Mountain Range, went ice climbing on a glacier in Seward, glimpsed her majesty, Denali, on a backpacking trip, and then said goodbye. This is the highlight reel. The 60 second synopsis that I recite when people ask me, "Alaska? What was that like?" But I skip over the in-between bits. The bits that are not as glamorous. The bits of loneliness in biking solo with my thoughts along the Chester Creek Trail. A protected bike path where the gray waters of the Cook Inlet hugged me on one side while sitka spruce, alders, and the occasional wandering moose lined the other. I gloss over the exhaustion in try-ing to jive with people at dimly lit bars for Meet-Up karaoke events. Making small talk over a pitchy rendition of Smash Mouth's "All Star" with folks who weren't necessarily my people. I fast-forward through the slow unfurling realization that I was deeply unhappy. And after a few months of surviving, I cut my time there short.

I leave out these parts of my experience because when I remember my isolation and sadness, I wonder what I could've done better. Never mind the fact that most people who move to a place without friends or family would also at times feel isolated. Never mind the fact that even fewer people would willingly place themselves in that situation at all and perhaps that's what I reflect on the most: should I have been there? And since my experience wasn't the fairytale that I had hoped for: what does that say about me? About my judgment?

I've reflected on the answers to these questions and the one that seems to emerge the most often is a disturbing notion of failure. I failed because my experience wasn't nonstop euphoria. I failed because in twelve weeks I didn't make the bonds of a lifetime. I failed because in deciding to live there instead of vacation for a week, I experienced the normal ebbs and flows of everyday life and the challenges of build-ing a community from scratch.

But failure is a harsh word. Unforgiving. If I treat my experience as a failure I'm doing myself and all that those months encompassed a disservice. Because those moments had joy and learning amidst the lulls and discomfort.

What I forget is that I did not travel to a new community because I thought it'd be easy. I traveled to be challenged and to learn a little bit more about who and what's inhabiting this world.

In the months after returning to the lower 48 (as the Alaskans say), there's a feeling in my chest of expansion. My notions of what Alaska and the communities—native and its colonizers (myself included) have been reexamined. I feel like Alice having stumbled out of the rabbit hole. When I look back, I realize that what I thought I would find was vastly different from what I actually experienced; the land more layered and varied than I ever could have imagined and will ever truly know.

It's humbling.

It's also a delightful notion as a human in the age of technology to find that videos on Youtube and Instagram are limited in their transmission of knowledge. What we see on our screens is curated by another and it's refreshing to know that reels can't replicate our lived experiences. I'm grateful to have been able to use my own lens to talk about the effects of climate change on Alaska's coastline and the intricacies of making beaver pelts with an oceanographer. I savor the words spoken in huffs between breaths about the complexities in oil drilling on Alaskan Native land as an attorney and I cycled below white dusted mountains. These conversations occurred with women who I eventually befriended in the weeks before I left.

Upon reflection, I've realized that human nature seems to allow discomfort to overshadow the fleeting joys and genuine connections that I made. But still, there are days when the triumphs push through and I think back to that same coastal trail when, on another solo bike ride, I was waved down by a man perched on a bench overlooking the marshlands. As I grinded my bike to a halt, he pointed to the inlet and said, "look." I followed his index finger to smooth humps creating trails in the gray waters. "They're belugas following a school of salmon," he said. I was delighted; I had never before seen a whale, and now I was watching a pod bobbing up and down in the sunset lit waters. Silently, we stood; two strangers awash in the scene. Around us the low call of the belugas reverberated, and then, from the wetlands, a Sandhill Crane took flight and stretched its giant ashy wings in the golden hour light. The man and I gazed in amazement; the bird soaring higher, the dark forms hugging the coastline, all of us moving deeper into the present.

A Moment

By Jannica Cuaresma Breslin

A moment

A glimpse of a lonesome astronomical passersby
A brief oneness with the universe
A humble understanding that you are but a mote in the macrocosm

A cold drop of rain from a sky billowing with mischief
An encouragement to share your umbrella and embody chivalry
Perhaps, a start of something delightful that inspires a smile even at
    the most mundane of times

A glance to the left and right
The preservation of the invaluable and irreplaceable
A gentle yet firm declaration that you are both knight and armor

A kiss hello
A show of gratitude for precious company
Perhaps, the first page of a new chapter that's been waiting to be
    given life

A call, a message in any sweet form
A bridge over time lost
A promise of consideration, kept

A decision to ignore a distraction or a thief in the guise of
urgent matter
A deep submergence into and within the present
A hyper-focus on those that have meaning and truth that endures
past anything that the mind can only try to grasp, meaning and
truth that can only be recognized by a heart that is willing to
stand weightless beneath a downpour of love

A moment

How many have you cherished?
How many have you wasted?

By Rosanne Shank

E ʻonipaʻa i ka ʻimi naʻauao

By Kapua Iao

Lydia Liliʻu Loloku Walania Wewehi Kamakaʻeha was born on September 2, 1838, to aliʻi nui Analea Keohokālole and high chief Caesar Kapaʻakea. After her birth, Liliʻu was hānai by Laura Konia and Abner Pākī, the parents of Bernice Pauahi Bishop who founded the Kamehameha Schools for Hawaiian keiki. Liliʻu was named heir to the throne in 1877. Then King David Laʻamea Kamananakapu Mahinulani Naloiaehuokalani Lumialani Kalākaua asked that she add "of the heavens/of the chiefs [-okalani]" to her name so that her status as crown princess was recognized. Liliʻuokalani became queen upon his death and was sworn in on January 29, 1891.

Queen Liliʻuokalani focused on restoring the powers of Hawaiians and the monarchy, which ultimately led to a coup, supported by the U.S. military, and her removal from the throne on January 17, 1893. After an unsuccessful uprising in 1895, in response to the takeover, Queen Liliʻuokalani was placed under house arrest at ʻIolani Palace. To protect those arrested after the uprising, she was forced to abdicate the throne on January 24, 1895.

The last Hawaiian monarch (first queen) is cherished for being a scholar, philanthropist, musician, and staunch supporter of Hawaiian culture. As a philanthropist, she especially focused on female-led organizations, such as the Queen's Hospital (founded in 1895 and still in use), the Ka'ahumanu Society (the oldest Hawaiian civic society today), and two banks established for women. An avid composer, Queen Lili'uokalani arranged numerous songs during her imprisonment such as "The Queen's Prayer" and "Ku'u Pua I Paoakalani." She also wrote and published her autobiography, *Hawai'i's Story by Hawai'i's Queen*, giving her account of the events and her appeals to the U.S. to restore Hawaiian monarchy.

Queen Lili'uokalani passed away on November 11, 1917, at the age of 79 but her legacy lives on in the music, her people (especially nā wāhine), and the continued fight for the return of the Kingdom of Hawai'i. Her motto "E 'onipa'a i ka 'imi na'auao," be steadfast in the seeking of knowledge, is typically shortened to onipa'a—to stand firm.

When I think about collective wisdom, belief, and faith, I think about all the strong Hawaiian women that came before me, from Queen Lili'uokalani and the women in her extended family to my grandmother, my aunties, my cousins, and my sister, and to all the women in Hawai'i I chose to surround myself with. I think about the past and how it informs the present and our future. The queen's life and her motto can be and must be remembered and followed even today. Even when friends and family and people and society tell you that you can't and you shouldn't, stand firm, onipa'a. Only you can choose your path.

Napkin Logic
By Ava Van Velsor

Ten Things I am most grateful for:
1. God conciousness and life
    beingness...in the now

2. Contentment
    simplicity of life

3. Freedom
    of the self created barriers

4. Bill
    Finding love and staying the course

5. Children/grands
    Love and be loved

6. Health
    Love of self

7. Minimalism
    An abundant life

8. Humanitarianism
    compassion and wonder

9. Array of experiences
    Gratefulness and future experiences

10. Healing
    centered and clear

Two Words: There's enough
Open up your fist and let your seeds drift on the wind
Once you leave the nest, sister, you can't go back again
Somewhere in between the beginning and the end
You're gonna find it

Recipe for One Heart's Emotional Healing

By Sam Anthony

Serves 1

When you lose someone, whether it's because they no longer walk this earth, or because they no longer walk this earth beside you, you experience several casualties. They have vacated your life, but perhaps the most perplexing aspect of it all is the loss of self. You've had no warning that you'll never see that person - the self you were in relation to them - again. They have been burnt on the pyre of an assumed future that you took for granted. As it all burns, you stand by, a ghost, mute, shell-shocked.

When all is said and done, all that is left in the wreckage is a pile of ashes, so small, so tender, so delicate. Ready to blow away in an instant. Yet as you watch, you notice that there is the faintest ember, flickering ever so feebly. This is the ember of your heart, and this most precious possession needs exquisite care.

Use this recipe as needed when facing a loss of any kind.

Ingredients:

1 lost human
1 part grief
1 part confused shock
1 part possibility

Step 1. Put the pieces of your former life in a blender. Turn it on high.

Step 2. Let the mixture rest. Set aside. There is no timeline. Patience is the most crucial kitchen tool here.

Step 3. Pull out your journal, pens, pencils, paints, brushes, and canvases. Explore the unique creativity that lives in you (yes, it's in everyone). Reflect. Rest. Ruminate.

Step 4. Tap into the web of humanity that has passed through the essential yet shatteringly human experience of being brought to your knees by loss. Talk about it. Talk some more. Repeat yourself. Gain clarity. Talk to close friends but also strangers. Feel held and supported by the fragile yet resilient human race.

Step 5. Join something. Be active. Leave your blended emotional slurry at home on your kitchen counter, continuing to rest. Run. Bike. Walk. Do yoga. Roller blade. Climb. Dance. Lift. Swim. Release the stored stress in your body and kick box your way out of the neverending pit of despair that you thought was your new home. As your external body gets stronger, so does your inner one.

Step 6. As emotions arise, invite them in the front door. Know that they will shift and change in unexpected ways, but only if you allow them their due course. They don't like to be ignored. If you do, they will fester.

Step 7. Eventually, the ember of your heart begins to grow brighter. There will be misfiring sparks and occasional pops and cracks as you become accustomed to your new normal. Celebrate the restarting of your heart. The fire burns, but differently this time.

Step 8. Follow the above steps as long as necessary. Trust the process. The only way out is through.

Pennies and Cardinals

By Anna Manning-Launius

I come from German, Irish, Norwegian heritage. We can be loud, opinionated, neat freaks and fiercely protective.

If you had to make a decision in our family you either just did it and heard about it, or you brought it to the table for everyone to talk it over. This usually consisted of my Gram calling the Aunts and Uncles to tell the others. Gramps over hearing and half smirking at Gram, Gram saying "OH, Pete." That was the norm, we all knew. Sometimes Gram brought it up just to squash any nay-sayers. It's possible she enjoyed the gossip too.

If you were with our Gram when the conversation took place, she'd have "her stick." I know of at least one sibling and a cousin or two that might have gotten a thump with it. If she didn't shake "her stick" at you, you'd hear her say, "It is what it is." Gramps would be nodding, thumbing his mustache. Then Gram would ask you if you wanted chicken and dumplings. Gramps would go to turn up the Cardinal's game. The decision had been made. It wasn't that they made the decision. It's just that the family had your back on the choice that you made.

Years later and my Gram and Gramps passed on to be our angels. Leaving pennies as reminders or sweet Cardinals flying by.

I'd messed up. Bad. There's bad and then there's what I did. I had to make a choice. Stay or go. No Gram and Gramps made it that much harder to carry. No pennies, no Cardinals. I felt like I had messed up so much that I didn't even deserve their love or God's grace.

Then it happened, the straw that broke the camel's back. I had to choose to be brave.

I wanted my boys to know what true strength looked like, real strength. I wanted them to know that receiving God's grace, love and mercy wasn't always pretty. Not photoshopped, filtered, perfectly folded, and everything put away (sorry Gramps). This choice was going to be scary, messy, untidy, crying myself to sleep, hard.

There wasn't an easy answer. Maybe that's how you know you are on the right path.

"Hard right over an easy wrong."

Take that step. That first one. The one that you know you must take. The one that keeps you up and brings your hands to shake.

Because.

You'll never have all the answers. There isn't going to be a perfect time. The list of what ifs will never stop.

My darling.

What if you don't? Isn't the not taking the step scarier than the freedom of a leap?

The leap. Take the leap, over and over again! Take the leap!

Be brave when life is rocky.

Today, tomorrow, now. Let go. Be free, strong, bold. You are more than enough. You are more than enough to receive God's grace, love and mercy. Always.

It is what it is.

Pennies and Cardinals.

Unkie's Prayer

By Jan Woodcock

Dear God,
I may not always know You,
But if You're anything like my uncle -
I love You.

And I am deeply grateful.

Grateful on this day, and in the last few months, especially,
For Francis Duane Allen, or Unkie, as my brothers and I called him.
For in him
We saw such a clear reflection of Your steadfast ways.

There, ready to be called on should we need you for anything.
Always there whether we even remembered to think of You or not

There with Your goodness and mercy
And Your overwhelming and abiding love

We have so much to thank You for on this day.
So many blessings have come our way,
we in this room who have been participants in,
and witnesses to, the well-lived life of Francis Allen

Asking that You take care of him now, doesn't quite seem quite right.
He so rarely needed much support
at least until his last days and weeks,
and You did send Iris,
who seemed to come from some heavenly place.

And if heaven is a place
I'm sure Unkie is there
Looking down upon all of this fuss being made over him
and shaking his head, yet loving this music and the people
And smiling in wonder at all the good memories being shared.
And experiencing a fair amount of incredulity at the big deal we are
    making here

But, he may also may be busy with other things,
like trying to find something useful to make out of those white,
    fluffy clouds
or strengthening the clarinet section of one of the angel bands
And making the bass section of the heavenly choir a bit more steady.

I'm thinking he's making sure everyone who wants it, gets some of
    his jams, relishes, dried fruit, and especially some of his latest
    home-brew.
And figuring out ingenious ways to fix little things for the angels
or comparing recipes for homemade bread with Jean and talking about
their kids, grandkids, and great grandkids.
and I'm sure she'll be introducing him to all the cool things they can
    discover in
the heavenly Institute for Continued Learning

I'm pretty sure he's volunteered to be on the crew that is tinkering
    with those golden gates so that more people can get in.

His life here on earth was rich and full.
Many times during his last weeks,
he said to us, without ever a trace of sadness
and with an irrepressible sense of delight and wonder
"I've had a good life. It's been a great ride. No regrets."

His life was full of love and goodness,
Of hard and productive work,
of acceptance of, and interest in others,
and of joy.

And so, God,
Having already been the beneficiaries of such love and joy
While it is difficult to let go,
we entrust him now to You

And we ask for Your blessing on each person in this room
And in all places this day
Help us to feel Your steady presence
Your understanding and forgiveness,
And Your delight in all that is good in us

So that we may carry Your goodness, Your patience, and
    Your kindness
Into places and to people who need it most.

We ask this so that we too, like Francis,
Can be in that number, of those who have come before
And who have found a way to act justly, be merciful, and walk
    humbly in the ways of You and of Your overwhelming and ever-
    lasting love.

Amen

2013

Week 41
____

By Robyn Maggio

It is 6:12 AM. My favorite time of day; the morning hours before the real start to my day. Before life becomes taken over by busyness. I have thirty-five minutes before the sun rises and light begins to seep through the clouds. I have no excuse for taking time to slow down and exchange worry for gratitude.

I sit on my meditation cushion wiggling my hips a little bit until I find my level of passable comfort. The only close by sound is the dripping and faint hum of my essential oil diffuser. With each gurgle it releases the scent of eucalyptus and peppermint, which as I inhale transports me to a forest of pine trees and crisp air. Another inhale and I am filled with a sense of calm, peace, and knowledge that I have an opportunity to align with my values. I can choose to love, to connect with the universe, and trust that each moment for the day will play out exactly as it is meant to be.

As my mind quiets, I feel the tension throughout my body also release. In my soul, I sense that I am right where I need to be. I release feeling lonely and disconnected, and just observe a passing sensation of wanting something more.

It is mornings like this that remind me that my life is exactly as God wants it to be. I am more than my thoughts and feelings. While they are valid, they do not have to be all encompassing or controlling. As I exhale, I let go breathing tension away and sit in the silence.

With each breath, I physically feel connected to a greater truth slowly revealing. I feel grounded in a sense of trust that the universe has my back. It is almost like being embraced and having that comfort, encouragement, even reassurance from someone else. Even though to someone glancing in the room I am alone, I feel surrounded find peace in knowing that friends, family, love, and hope, are always with me.

With a final exhale, I become more aware of my physical body. Through my closed eyes I can see it is starting to be brighter. Right on cue, I hear a cheery bird chirp, blink my eyes open, and see the darkness turn to light as the sun rises. What a wonderful start to another beautiful day.

Nowhere without light
By Gwen Van Velsor

It's easy to love the mountains and mossy forests and gentle streams
Crashing waves and clip of rain on glassy lake
But if God is everywhere,
then God is everywhere
in your neighbor's mouth
in the moonbeam between dirty blinds
in the laughter behind a window screen
in the colorful weeds growing up in the cracks of parking lots
in the footsteps and the chewing gum and the dollar tortillas
in hands
in dirty water
in blue jay skies
in blood
in salted dough
in the humming, heart beating silence of sleep and shared dreams
in the skyline full of flat and glimmering rooftops
in songbirds on the line, a God who speaks
a seed in the belly of the bird will be a city, and it will be good

a dense place where God's heart beats with a deafening fervor so
    loud you can't mistake it for
noise

By Jannica Cuaresma Breslin

I see you, I hear you, I understand you
Little bird, don't you see?
You are a magnificent eagle
With majestic wings
And potential to soar higher than the clouds

When you feel out of place,
Don't apologize for existing
Your individuality complements others,
Empowers others
You have your divine seat on this earth
You are a note, integral to the symphony that is the world

When you are lost in others' words and actions,
Carve your own path in the universe
Be your own navigator
Greet the stars with enthusiasm and sail to the constellations
That call to your soul and beyond

When you feel incomplete or broken,
Have faith that when you reach out,
Even in darkness,
That I will take your hand
Have faith that I will lend you parts of myself
To help make you whole

When you feel like you have grief that is too much to bear,
Be brave enough to be generous and share your burden with those
    who are never scarce whenever you were in need
Surrender to the elements around you
Melt in them
Let them mourn with you
And breathe
Keep breathing
Keep breathing
Keep breathing

When failures have pushed you down onto the ground
And your face is drowning in mud,
Get back up,
Wipe your tears,
Dust off your crown,
Wash your regal clothes,
And remember that while you may be all of the worst
Parts of your family tree,
You are also all of the best
And give love to yourself,
For you are worthy of love
Always

By Jessica Cho Johnston

When I read Crying in H-Mart I didn't expect to identify with it
So much
H-Mart was giving away calendars,
thought I'd cook my way through some of the Korean recipes

didn't expect to lose my dad a couple of months later

my dad would have loved
Kimchi Rice Cake Soup with Dumplings

Here's to you dad, Japche
my sad attempt at perfectly cooked and julienned eggs, he would
    have laughed at our undercooked noodles
but we tried and it was tasty

Chicken katsu-Dan
Dad would have shook his head at the air fryer
but it was delicious

Who knew mung beans were so versatile

When I was little this would come out with Korean BBQ and I'd ask
    my dad what it was
He thought some kind of Jelly fish
Mystery solved dad
it's mung bean starch AKA sesame oil flavored vegan gelatin

Flower Korean Egg Roll
This was an official food fail but we had fun trying
My dad and I loved fish, even smelly mackerel
this fish sausage may have been a bridge too far
for even him

Happy birthday daddy
He would have been 69 today
So I pulled the oxtails out of the freezer
for the next time he came to visit and made one of his favorite soups
I think he would have approved
we love and miss you

He was supposed to be here today
We were all supposed to be together
but we aren't and it's heartbreaking
Love you always

Spiritual Pruning

By Mary Speace

runing. Spiritual pruning.

What do you all think of when you think of pruning? What visual do you have in your mind? I think of an arborist or vinedresser coming out with shears, wrapping the blades around a dead or fruitless branch and then he or she closes down on the handles and off comes the branch. Sometimes it's easy and it falls right to the ground, but other times, it takes a lot of energy. Some branches are more stubborn than others.

So I want to dig deeper into what it means for our lives, our hearts, to be pruned. In John 15, it says, "I am the true vine, and my Father is the vinedresser. Every branch in me that does not bear fruit he takes away, and every branch that does bear fruit he prunes, that it may bear more fruit."

But before we get started, let me give a little background on John 15. Jesus is giving the last of His many "I am's," and nearing the end of what we call his Farewell Discourse before He leaves to pay the ultimate sacrifice. So far, He is the Bread of Life, the Light of the World, the Good Shepherd, the Resurrection, the Way, the Truth and the Life and now He is the True Vine and His Father, the Vinedresser.

In John 15 and preceding chapters, He wants to make sure to remind his disciples of the essential truths that will guide and sustain them once He is no longer with them. And in John 15, the analogy of the vine and branches is one part of that. It is important to note that this is not the first time that the vineyard is used as an analogy. The Old Testament frequently uses the vineyard or vine as a symbol for Israel. In Isaiah 5:1-7, it reads "he looked for it to yield grapes, but it yielded wild grapes." Here God is depicted as the vinedresser, but he is only awarded with wild grapes due to Israel's disobedience. The problem is that the vine of Israel lacks the intended fruitfulness. But now praise God, Jesus is the answer and has fulfilled God's intended promise. Here the fruitfulness of Christ is contrasted with the fruitlessness of Israel. We are given a redeemer, a second chance. We can now have a fruitful life in Christ as the new and True Vine. But we must stress the importance of what that "in Christ" means. Abiding in Christ refers to those that have first accepted Christ as their Savior. It is for believers, those that remain in Him, are rooted in Him. The one who abides in Christ will have life and not death; the one who abides in Christ will be answered, and the one who abides in Christ will have fullness of joy.

So once we know we are rooted in Christ, and have a growing vine with many branches, how do we keep our vine and our branches healthy? How do we nourish our vine so that it can bear much fruit? Well, in John 15, God's answer is to prune our branches, but how and what does that mean?

I am going to walk you through a little bit of my last year and the extensive pruning season God has led me through. I've learned a lot and it is at times hard to put into words and difficult to talk about, but I can say faith without seasons of pruning and sanctification is really no faith at all because **spiritual pruning produces an abundant life** by removing that which prevents spiritual growth. It is the essential, but at times painful, process that rids us of ourselves.

Spiritual Pruning Exposes Sin

By Mary Speace

Pruning exposes sin. This addresses the dead limbs in verse 2 **(John 15:1-17)** that are cut off completely. There is no fruit or foliage growing on these branches. This is a tough one for me (actually the second point is too, but we'll get to that). You see the hard part is that exposing sin reveals misplaced trust and most of us don't like how uncomfortable that makes us feel. We consistently choose to place our hope and trust in something other than in God. Sin is where we either consciously, or subconsciously, say, "more of me, God, and less of you." And coming to terms with that is painful. It's humbling. It's the point where our allegiance is revealed. And these branches are dead because there is no life in them whatsoever, because Christ has been pushed out of the way completely. Let me give you an example.

Early last year, in January 2021, I got up from the couch quickly to tend to one of my kids, and I felt an instant, sharp pain in my back, right to the left of my spine. It felt like a knot. I tried to roll it out, but it only made it hurt more. So I chose to ignore it, like I do most of the time, but the pain continued to get worse and began to shoot down my back, around my hip and down the front of my leg. I am an intensive care nurse and work long 12 hour shifts, sometimes I never even get the chance to sit down, so those shifts often made the pain worse. After my shifts, I could barely walk to my car, limping and fighting back the tears. Working out had become nonexistent because it was too painful. But of course, I kept going into work. It wasn't until the middle of March, that I could barely walk, barely stand to cook or dry my hair. My days were long. I honestly wanted to cry most of the time. So I said enough was enough and I got an MRI. Turns out I had a herniated disc in my back that was pushing on my femoral nerve, causing excruciating pain that around the clock ibuprofen could barely touch. I sought out many therapies and treatments before considering surgery. Some helped, some didn't. It was months of pain and many bottles of ibuprofen. This pain started as physical pain, but then it spread. It destroyed my morale and my joy. My temper was short. It made me feel incapable of everything, not just physically, but more so mentally, emotionally and spiritually. Relationships were strained with my kids, friends, family and my husband.

So why do I tell you this when we're on the topic of sin? I share this with you because it wasn't the physical pain that caused me to sin. For example, it wasn't the pain that caused me to lash out in anger at my husband or kids. It wasn't the pain that caused me to wallow in self-pity. Sin had subtlety been at work years prior and the pain had been used to expose it. God was using this pain to completely empty me of myself, to reveal the many areas of idol worship in my life. Now I am not here to dwell on the causation of the pain, but God is our vinedresser, so God may have caused the pain in my life as a result of the pruning process, or He may not have and just chose to use the pain to reveal branches that needed pruning. But either way He was going to use it for my good and my spiritual growth.

It became clear to me that control was an idol in my life. And if the circumstances of my life were in control, I felt contentment and if they weren't, I felt despair. There were many idols, things that I often put my trust in rather than God. I put my trust in my health. I put my trust in my finances. I put my trust in well-behaved kids and a clean home.

I put my trust in my work and performance. I put my trust in being a good mother, the perfect wife. And I put my trust in my husband to fulfill me. And what this pain revealed is that when one of those is out of my control, my world falls apart, and by world, I mean my peace, my joy, my patience, my love for others, and my love for myself. Do you see where I'm going?

Sin infects. Sin spreads quickly. Much like a plant, if dead limbs remain, they are an entry point for disease or rot or insects to take over and kill it. Sin left unchecked works in a very similar fashion, extending its control over every part of a Christian's life. Put simply, sin kills. In other words, sin prevents spiritual growth. I definitely resonated with this over the past year. The hard part with the sin I was dealing with was that it was so intangible. It wasn't something I could wrap my hands around. It couldn't be fixed by changing my physical habits alone. The worship of this false state of perfection and control had penetrated every area of my life leaving me angry, jealous, bitter, and depressed. It had penetrated my soul and became difficult to pinpoint my sin.

I read this in a book titled Fruit of Christ's Presence by Harry Lee Poe while preparing for this message:

> "It is easier to recognize 'all my sins' than to face the fact that I am a jealous person. It is easier to confess 'all my sins' than to confess self-pity. It is easier to acknowledge 'all my sins' in theory than to deal with a single one specifically. As long as sin is nameless and faceless, we can continue to ignore it. Jesus said that when the Holy Spirit came He would convince the world of sin (John 16:8). Jesus knew that people do not want to face the fact of sin, even if it means their own self-destruction. Simply put, we do not want our sins exposed. If we willingly gave up our sins, the pruning would not be as painful."

So rather than confessing sin, we tolerate it, even ignore it. So my question here is, how do we participate in the process of exposing our sin? Is it an active or passive process? I would argue it is an active process. We need to pray the difficult prayer for sin to be exposed in our lives. Being rooted and abiding in Him is essential to this process and why we spoke about it last night. The things that helped me and continue to help me are seeking out friends to pray for me, talking openly with my husband, seeking biblical counseling, and spending time in the Word and in prayer. I don't wake up early every morning to read my bible and pray just because I hate sleep and I love to see the dark. It's because I can't afford not to! My daily fight for time in the Word is the single, most important habit of getting through this past year. Hands down. Being in the Word is how I stay rooted in Christ and how God speaks to me.

This process for me has not been easy, though. It actually has been really painful at times. It's been a lot of up and downs, emotionally and spiritually. Days where I feel spiritually so strong, where His Word is so active in my heart and mind. Where I can battle every lie or bad thought and other days, where I struggle to see the truth. I struggle to believe that His strength is really made perfect in my weakness. I struggle to believe that He is actually working for my good. I struggle to consider it joy when I face many trials. I struggle to believe that He is able when I am not. But then I am reminded faith is not supported by my emotions alone. When I struggle to believe these truths it is because I am not abiding in Jesus. In John 15 and countless other areas of the bible, including 1 John, it stresses the importance of abiding, which means to remain steadfast. It says "Abide in me, and I in you" and later, "apart from me, you can do nothing." I say it again, abiding is not a passive process. It requires action on our part. There is a reason spiritual disciplines are called disciplines. It's because it's not easy. It requires our physical, emotional, and mental fervor. It's no reason why I struggle to believe or fight the emotional battle when I am not abiding.

So how should we respond when it's hard? My husband often has to remind me to manage my expectations. Manage my expectations with every military move, with parenting, with work, and with faith. We all know that being in Christ is not synonymous with happiness and ease in life, but yet we still find ourselves upset or pouting or angry when life isn't happy or easy. But James reminds us that every trial is an opportunity for spiritual growth and I think our perspective when in the midst of trials and pruning is misaligned. I think if we wake up every day knowing that the day probably won't go exactly as planned or with incredible ease, we may be able to handle it better.

For example, I have no idea what kind of kid I am going to get when they wake up. Teachers, you have no idea what kind of kids you're going to get when you get to school. I could get a phone call tonight with devastating news, a family member might be diagnosed with a terminal illness, or a job with its financial provision could be lost. We just don't know, but our reaction to those hard things starts with the health of our abiding. Our reaction to being pruned must be to endure in abiding. We need to look at pruning as an opportunity for God to be at work in our lives, and not as a punishment.

The same book I mentioned above writes it this way:

> "Christians seem surprised that spiritual pruning may be painful. Freedom from pain and suffering is a promise of a Christian's *future glorification*, but pain and suffering are a part of *present sanctification*. The pain of spiritual pruning is a result of our reluctance to give up whatever inhibits our growth. Christians do not like to be pruned. It hurts. Whenever the Lord prunes us, we lose a part of ourselves. Habits, attitudes, and thoughts are as much a part of us as our faces, arms, and legs. To have part of our spiritual being pruned is to lose part of who we are. *But without the pruning, we remain all foliage and no fruit.*"

So because I am getting long winded here, simply put, pruning of dead limbs is the pruning of the sin in our lives that so easily can infect and prevent the growth of fruit in our lives. It is a painful, but necessary part of abiding and growing in Christ. If you are effectively abiding and growing in Christ, expect to be pruned.

Spiritual Pruning Confronts Complacency

By Mary Speace

Pruning confronts complacency. Yeah, this is a hard pill to swallow too. If some of you are fidgeting in your chair right now, it's okay. I have fidgeted as well and often still am. This point derives from verse 2 (**John 15:1-17**) as well, "and every branch that does bear fruit he prunes, that it may bear more fruit." Complacent branches are those branches that are still alive, but those ones that have not born much fruit, if any at all, but still have leaves present. The leaves are pretty, but when you or a friend or your child or your spouse walk up to the tree for a grape, they may leave with empty hands. The scary part about complacency is that it can go unnoticed for quite some time because your tree may still have some fruit, but maybe it's not as satisfying. Maybe the fruit isn't as sweet or as big as it could be. Maybe it doesn't feed as many as it used to.

This one hit me hard and honestly this is very humbling and difficult to talk about because this has left me feeling ashamed or envious of someone else's fruitful branches. And I will talk about how shame and envy are not the intended consequences of pruning, but shame and/or envy may be something you are experiencing today or may face in the future and I want to help replace those lies with truth and grace.

Remember how I said that my physical pain exposed idols in my life. Well, the pain also forced me to realize how much comfort and security I receive from those things I am gifted in. I find comfort in my abilities and in perfect, ideal circumstances. After having kids, I have tried to avoid pain and stress because with kids I feel like I have enough of it. I actually pursue circumstances that bring about the least amount of discomfort. It's not that I don't enjoy to work hard, but I often find it painful and uncomfortable to work hard at something that takes up a lot of my time and effort, especially those things that I am not naturally gifted at. It's easy to continue to pursue those things that use our gifts, but harder to pursue those things that expose and strengthen our weaknesses. Now I am not saying not to use your gifts, but I am saying to not rely solely on your gifts and neglect strengthening your weaknesses.

I recently read the book *Deeply Formed Life* by Rich Villodas. And there was a very challenging anecdote that he shared. In seminary, he had to give a presentation on a book, but because he was well versed in the topic of the book, he didn't read it, but gave the presentation anyway. And in the middle of his presentation, his professor stopped him and said, "you didn't read the book, did you?" He responded no and the professor asked that he still continue and finish his presentation, but afterward, the professor said, "Rich, you have a gift to give a presentation by just reading the dust cover, but you also have a curse. The curse is you will be tempted to believe you can live off your gifts and not do the deep work of character formation. Your gifts can only take you so far. But there are no such limits when there is a life marked by deep character." Rich goes on to say that we often fail to be deeply formed and rather settle for being shallowly shaped. This is what I am talking about when I say that pruning confronts complacency. God does not desire us to be shallowly shaped by the passive influences of our daily life. That may be the countless hours we spend on social media, tv, or just plain apathy towards all things that prevent us from getting up off the hypothetical couch. He desires to bear fruit in us, and not just for your consumption, but for others as well.

We need to get real and pray about the areas of our lives that we say, "not right now, Lord. I'm too tired. I just can't. That is way too hard. I don't have time." I understand it's hard; I have said every single one of these things, but we still need to prioritize our relationship with Him and respond with His Word and remember Philippians 4:13 that says "I can do all things through Christ who strengthens me," or Galatians 2:20, "It is no longer I who live, but Christ who lives in me."

For example, writing this message definitely took me out of my comfort zone. While I love reading the Word, I don't always love the stress of translating my knowledge into a comprehensive message. The lesson learned for me here is that I don't enjoy the things that provoke fear, discomfort or stress. It happens at work too. When a new patient comes in that is "crashing" or very sick, I quietly hope that I'm not the nurse to get them. Most often then, I end up getting that patient. And why do I feel this way? And why do some of you feel this way? I think we all subconsciously want to avoid those things that:

1. Don't make us look good.
2. Create a lot of work.
3. Take up time or space.
4. Force us to be vulnerable.

What's inherently wrong with all these initial responses? They freeze us up. They create stagnancy and prevent the bearing of fruit. So let's play this out. If I never took that really sick patient, how then am I supposed to learn that I actually can do it or that it's okay to learn from my mistakes or how I can improve next time? If I never overcame that fear of speaking in front of people, you wouldn't be hearing these truths that God has laid on my heart countless times to share with you. There has been a heavy burden for quite some time now to share this message. And so many times I've tried to get out of it. I first asked some friends, then I prayed for a friend from college to come as a guest speaker. Why? Fear. Fear that can be so crippling it forces me to curl up, cry, pout, and scream, "I can't do it!"

We learn as a result of facing our fears and strengthening our weaknesses! We learn who Christ is in us when we choose to admit we are unable, but He is more than able! YOU learn who Christ is in YOU when YOU choose to admit YOU are unable, but He is more than able!

There were seasons of my life where I would have tried to keep up an image, where I didn't read my bible, and where I didn't pray in months. And guess what? Those months, years were pretty dry and they certainly didn't help me once the pain hit last January. They were the complacent branches on my vine that desperately needed to be pruned. God couldn't wait to prune those stubborn branches. I know He is going to rejoice and get the glory with all the fruit He is going to bear as a result of this season, as well your season of pruning.

In light of this, I want to return to the idea of shame and envy that can come when we realize our vine is bearing no fruit and others' branches are. When I read John 15 months ago, I first felt an overwhelming amount of sadness and shame when I realized I didn't see any spiritual fruit in my life. I waffle back and forth sometimes into still feeling shame or disgust that my actions or lack of fruit have consequences to my faith and on others. But I consistently am reminded of His grace. Ephesians 2:8 says, "for by grace I have been saved and it is not my doing, but the gift of God." 2 Corinthians 12:9 says, "His grace is sufficient for me and His power made perfect in my weakness." Hebrews 4:16 says, "to draw near to the throne of grace with confidence…to help us in our time of need." And Psalm 73:26 says, "My flesh and my heart may fail, but God is the strength of my heart and my portion forever."

What is the resounding theme here? When we feel shame, it's because the focus is on ourselves and not Christ. When I feel shame, I know I am so focused on myself and have completely lost sight of the Gospel. We can so easily forget, which is why again abiding in God's Word is the single most important way to refocus our hearts and minds. The Word of God is like a cleansing agent. It cleanses us of sin and inspires holiness and bears fruit like it says in John 15:3.

Spiritual Pruning Bears Fruit

By Mary Speace

Pruning bears fruit and I may even add, it nourishes the vine. The main point I want to stress here is that the vinedresser's number one goal is a healthy, fruitful plant and we need to trust the vinedresser. Even if we can't see past the pain, He can. He sees the end result. He sees the plant's potential in good and bad ways and knows which branches can stay and which need to go. He wants to rid us of those dead and fruitless branches so that we can bear more fruit.

I read that the Greek word _airo_ for "takes away" in verse 2 (John 15:1-17) is better translated as to lift up. The analogy here is that, those low hanging, weighted branches can't see the sun (or light) and crowd the plant, thus affecting the growth of the whole plant. So the vinedresser either trims them to lift them up or cut them altogether so that the plant is less weighted and less crowded. This way, more of the plant will get sunlight thus producing more fruit. What I want you to see is that the pruning process is not just for our benefit, it's for the benefit of others as well.

In review, **spiritual pruning produces an abundant life** by removing that which prevents spiritual growth. We discussed how pruning exposes sin, confronts complacency and bears fruit. All these things root and connect us to the True Vine of Christ. And when cleansed and watered with His Word, we help to fulfill God's plan and purposes.

Before closing, I want to remind you of this. Spiritual growth requires us to abide, and abiding takes action. It takes spiritual pruning and again it is not a passive process. It takes desire. It takes persistence. But the motivation must come from loving Christ more than we love ourselves. There is a reason why the branches are connected to the vine. They can't survive without it. We can't survive without it, that being Christ.

I know it's not easy and you might be saying, I'm tired; These kids monopolize all my time; My job takes all my time; This past sin issue is just too much to overcome and I can't forgive myself or someone else; The pain from past trauma is too difficult to face, to forgive. There is a list of things. And the truth is, you can't will yourself to forgive. You can't will yourself to stop feeling the pain. But there is someone who can, and his name is Jesus. We have the ultimate example! Christ already took on the pain of this world for you. Christ already loved the unlovable for you. And if you don't have a relationship with him, today can be that day. And if you do have a relationship with Jesus, but don't feel close to Him, I encourage you to ask yourself some questions, to examine where you're at spiritually. What's holding you back?

Also, reach out. Verse 12 (**John 15:1-17**) says, "this is my commandment, that you love another as I have loved you. Greater love has no one than this, that someone lay down his life for his friends." I guarantee there is someone that you can seek out and say, "I need prayer. I need help getting and keeping my feet under me." I have done that so many times. I can give you a few examples. Months ago in the thick of the pain, I called a few women and said, "I need prayer. I feel so weak." And one friend, Amanda said, "actually, all I see, Mary, is strength. Asking for help makes you strong and that is a great place to start." I will never forget that. Another time, I texted Kate and said, "today is a bad day. I need prayer. I can't push this boulder up the hill any longer." And she said, "you've helped me in a season where I was weak and thankfully now, I am in a season where I have enough energy to help push that boulder up with you. You're not alone." And when I was struggling being in the Word on a daily basis, I called up a mentor, Lynelle, and asked that she check in on me every morning to ask what I'm learning in my quiet time. And Kathryn and I have more conversation before 6 o'clock in the morning than most people do throughout a day. She consistently asks how I'm doing, how she can pray for me, and does it. And there are countless other women in my life who encourage me. Why do all these woman do this for me? Because they care and they know it's a commandment to love their friends. My point in sharing these things is that it's okay to admit you don't have it all together. We don't do it enough, and we need to support one another as we abide in Christ together. We need to accept where God has us right now, confess that we want to learn more, and then get after it. There is no shame, no condemnation in Christ.

I leave you with this verse. Hebrews 12:1-3

> "Therefore since we are surrounded by such a great cloud of witnesses, let us also lay aside every weight, and sin which clings so closely, and let us run with endurance the race that is set before us, looking to Jesus, the founder and perfecter of our faith, who for the joy that was set before him endured the cross, despising the shame, and is seated at the right hand of the throne of God. Consider him who endured from sinners such hostility against himself, so that you may not grow weary or fainthearted."

By Carol Clupny

"*I* am glad I have a friend like you" wrote Dixie a few days ago. "I am too," I responded.

"Do you remember when we met? The night I called you? I was home, alone, late at night. I told you I lived here in Oregon which I had to teach you to pronounce. You acted like you never heard of the State of Oregon and made me convince you it existed."

You were at your home, in the countryside of Georgia a couple thousand miles away. But as I recall, we were actually in the same place, in the city called Despair. It was dark there, with no streetlamps to light our way. We both were on the internet and discovered each other had reached out to a social media site, the one where the late night parkies hang out, hoping to find someone with a lantern to light the way to our answers.

I said, "if I lived closer, I would show up at your door with a bottle of Pendleton OREGON whiskey and two shot glasses. We would turn up the music and dance in your living room." We both laughed at the vision of this incredible dance party.

I felt your hand that night, Dixie, reaching across the miles and taking mine. And I reached back across the miles and took your other hand. And we have been holding hands for a long time now. I will never tire of it.

"If you ever need to hear a voice in the middle of the night
When it seems so black outside that you can't remember light
Ever shone on you or the ones you love in this or another lifetime
And the voice you need to hear is the true and the trusted kind
With a soft familiar rhythm in these swirling unsure times"
From *This is Love* by Mary Chapin Carpenter

My world circles the sun each year. I age away in years, 12 years since my diagnosis. The friendship of those living close to me has thinned. Their ranks have been strengthened by others from a distance. I have been nourished by words, poetry, writing, art, dance, humor.

I am content, happy, and some days filled with joy. I never used to be that way. I was an angry youth. I complicated my life with unhealthy relationships. But I always had a goal.

The anger didn't leave me when I grew up. And when Parkinsons came I stuffed it down inside like I had so many other things. And the anger didn't start to go away until I knelt on a dusty road on the Camino in Spain. And it wasn't gone even after I broke open my heart walking in France. Talk therapy, medication, and changing my life practices changed me.

I am not afraid. I am not guilty. I am at peace. I choose joy. I change my adversities into adventures.

I keep chanting my mantra of hope. Each day I set out to have the best day of my life. Time. It heals.

"If you ever need some proof that time can heal your wounds
Just step inside my heart and walk around these rooms
Where the shadows used to be
You can feel as well as see how peace can hover
Now time's been here to fix what's broken with its power."
From This is Love by Mary Chapin Carpenter

For Beloved

By Jannica Cuaresma Breslin

I feel my chest caving in,
As the void your loss has spawned
Sucks in so much of who I used to be
When you were still with me
My melancholy heart is losing rhythm,
Losing voice, losing vigor
Every beat is like a strum
Of a chord that is missing a note,
Strings untuned,
Unable to create sound
That is comprehensible
And delightful to the soul
Yet, because I loved you
And I love you still,
I harvest good thoughts, the best,
Though the climate is unfitting
I remember every arch and line
In your slender contour;
Every shade of black and white
In every silk-strand of hair;

Every glimmer of silver and onyx
In your eyes, sheathed in clashing
Desire to be wanted and need to protect;
Every scar heralding courage;
And every moment of heightened senses
Shared between you and me
Because I will continue to
Keep you in my mind and heart,
I am believing that you are,
Now and forevermore,
Liberated from all earthly burdens,
Enveloped in joy not bound by mortal limits,
And that you do and always will,
Like I do and always will with yours,
Deep down to the very core of your essence,
Know that my love for you is
Simple and infinite

DNA

By Gwen Van Velsor

The writing in our blood is never broken down
Recycled in the dust of the earth
We are eternal
Each breath a gift from someone before
Stories braided into every strand of hair
You are made up of ancestral nucleotides
You are eternal
The steps I make are mapped in my bones
Traveling to the summit of my daughter's mountain
And to the bottom of her daughter's ocean
Raining on the sacred land of those who come after
I am eternal

By

www.ingramcontent.com/pod-product-compliance
Lightning Source LLC
Chambersburg PA
CBHW072238150726
48002CB00005B/2150